quick **breads**

quick breads

Linda Collister photography by Kate Whitaker

RYLAND
PETERS
& SMALL

LONDON NEW YORK

Senior Designer Steve Painter
Editor Ann Baggaley
Production Gemma Moules
Publishing Director Alison Starling
Index Hilary Bird

Food stylists Linda Tubby and
  Sunil Vijayakar
Props stylist Róisín Nield

**The author would like to thank the
following for their help:**
Barbara Levy, Julia Charles, Kate
Whitaker, Steve Painter, Ann Baggaley,
Linda Tubby, Róisín Nield, and Alan Hertz

First published in the
United States in 2007
by Ryland Peters & Small, Inc
519 Broadway, 5th Floor
New York, NY 10012
www.rylandpeters.com

10 9 8 7 6 5 4 3 2 1

Text © Linda Collister 2007
Design and photographs
© Ryland Peters & Small 2007

Printed in China

ISBN-13: 978 1 84597 475 6
ISBN-10: 1 84597 475 1

Library of Congress Cataloging-in-
Publication Data

Collister, Linda.
  Quick breads / Linda Collister ;
photography by Kate Whitaker.
      p. cm.
  Includes index.
  ISBN 978-1-84597-475-6
  1.   Bread.   I. Title.
  TX769.C566 2007
  641.8'15--dc22

2007011475

Notes
• All spoon measurements are level unless
otherwise specified.
• Ovens should be preheated to the
specified temperatures. All ovens work
slightly differently. I recommend using
an oven thermometer and suggest you
consult the maker's handbook for any
special instructions—particularly if you are
using a convection oven as you may need
to adjust cooking temperatures according
to the manufacturer's instructions.

contents

6 making bread the easy way

8 savory breads

28 cornbreads

34 breakfast breads

50 small breads

64 index

making bread the easy way

Anyone can enjoy their own homemade bread, warm and wonderful from the oven. You don't need baking expertise to make these quick breads. The ingredients are mixed briefly, then baked—there's no kneading, no waiting for the dough to rise. A loaf can be ready for the oven in under 15 minutes.

In this book you will find quick breads to eat with a bowl of soup, a chunk of cheese, a spoonful of jam, or just a pat of good butter; savory loaves to accompany a meal; and fruity loaves for a sweet treat. The recipes use good quality organic flours— stone-ground varieties like rye, spelt, whole-wheat, and cornmeal. Nuts, seeds, herbs and spices, and fresh and dried fruits add texture as well as excellent flavor. The doughs are enriched with free-range eggs, unsalted butter, or olive oil. In many recipes, milk, buttermilk, or plain yogurt add a delicious tang and give the crumb a moist lightness. Those old-fashioned kitchen-cupboard staples baking powder and baking soda are used to raise the breads. (It's vital not to overdo the given quantities of these ingredients, as instead of making your breads bigger and lighter you will end up with yellow dough and an unpleasant fizzy flavor.)

Most of the breads are at their best eaten straight from the oven, or on the same day, but some improve with keeping for a day or two before slicing and many freeze well.

savory **breads**

A rustic loaf flavored with fresh sage, this is good served warm from the oven to accompany hearty winter soups and stews.

Tuscan fresh sage and olive oil bread

3 cups unbleached all-purpose flour

1 cup whole-wheat flour

2 teaspoons chopped fresh sage leaves

1 tablespoon baking powder

½ teaspoon sea salt

2 extra-large eggs

3 tablespoons olive oil

about ¾ cup milk (not fat-free)

a baking sheet, lightly greased

Makes 1 medium loaf

Preheat the oven to 350°F.

Mix the flours with the chopped sage, baking powder, and salt in a large bowl.

In a separate bowl, lightly beat the eggs with the olive oil and milk, then stir into the dry ingredients to make a soft and slightly sticky dough. If there are dry crumbs or the dough feels stiff, work in a little more milk.

Turn out the dough onto a lightly floured surface and shape into a ball about 7 inches across. Set on the baking sheet and score the top with a knife.

Put in the oven immediately and bake for about 45 minutes until golden brown and the loaf sounds hollow when tapped underneath with your knuckles. Transfer to a wire rack and leave until cool enough to break into quarters or cut into thick slices. This loaf is best eaten the same day but can be frozen for up to 1 month.

Variation: Olive and rosemary bread
This bread has plenty of flavor. Use the best olives you can find—green, black, or a mix—and fresh rosemary, and enjoy with soup and salad.

To make the loaf, follow the method above, replacing the sage with 1 teaspoon chopped fresh rosemary and adding ½ cup roughly chopped black and green olives.

This German recipe from my friend Brigitte makes a loaf that looks more like a mosaic of seeds, nuts, and grains than bread. It is dense and very nutritious, good with butter and honey, soft cheeses, and salads. It is also very adaptable—the wheat flakes can be replaced with rye flakes, the walnuts with chopped almonds, cashews, or toasted pine nuts.

seedy loaf

2 cups wheat germ, or wheat germ and wheat bran mix

¾ cup wheat flakes

1 cup walnut pieces

⅓ cup sunflower seeds

⅓ cup pumpkin seeds

¼ cup sesame seeds

¼ cup flaxseed

1¼ cups bulghur wheat or cracked wheat

1 teaspoon baking soda

1 teaspoon sea salt

1 extra-large egg

2 tablespoons honey

2 cups plain yogurt (not fat-free)

a 9 x 5 x 3-inch loaf pan, well greased and base-lined with parchment paper

Makes 1 large loaf

Put the wheat germ and flakes, walnuts, seeds, bulghur, baking soda, and salt into a large bowl. Stir with a wooden spoon until thoroughly combined.

In a small bowl, beat the egg with the honey and yogurt, then mix into the dry ingredients. Let soak for 30 minutes.

Meanwhile, preheat the oven to 350°F.

Stir the bread mixture thoroughly, then scrape into the prepared pan and spread evenly. Bake for 30 minutes then cover loosely with foil or parchment paper to prevent overbrowning and cook for 25 minutes more. Test the loaf is cooked by pushing a skewer into the center—if it comes out clean the loaf is ready. If the skewer comes out sticky with dough, cook for a further 5 minutes and test again.

Carefully turn out onto a wire rack, remove the lining paper, and let cool completely before slicing. Wrap well and eat within 2 days, or toast. Not suitable for freezing.

Rolled oats give this bread a nice chewy texture and the molasses adds a pleasant but not overwhelming tang. This loaf slices well for sandwiches, is great toasted for breakfast, and keeps for a couple of days.

molasses oatmeal loaf

2 tablespoons molasses

1⅓ cups buttermilk

¾ cup rolled oats

1⅔ cups whole-wheat flour

1¾ cups unbleached all-purpose flour

1 teaspoon baking soda

1 teaspoon sea salt

2 tablespoons unsalted butter, chilled and cut into cubes

1 extra-large egg, beaten

an 8 x 4 x 2½-inch loaf pan, well greased

Makes 1 medium loaf

Mix the molasses and the buttermilk in a large bowl. Stir in the oats then let soak for 30 minutes.

Preheat the oven to 400°F.

In another bowl, mix the flours, baking soda, and salt. Add the pieces of butter and rub in, using the tips of your fingers, until the mixture looks like fine crumbs.

Add the beaten egg and the mixture of soaked oats and mix well with a wooden spoon to make a fairly heavy dough. Scrape the mixture into the greased loaf pan and with floured fingers press it into a neat loaf shape.

Bake for 10 minutes then reduce the oven temperature to 350°F and bake for a further 35 minutes.

Turn out the loaf onto a wire rack and let cool to room temperature before slicing.

Keep tightly wrapped and eat within 3 days, or toast. Can be frozen for up to 1 month.

This moist, well-flavored loaf can be made with either caraway seeds for "New York"-style rye or cumin seeds for a Scandinavian taste. Whichever you choose, the flavor is best the day after baking. The bread is good thinly sliced and served with smoked fish, gravadlax, pickled herring, or salami, or toasted for breakfast. Rye flour and rye flakes are available in larger supermarkets and natural food stores.

quick rye bread

3 cups rye flour

3 tablespoons rye flakes, plus extra for sprinkling

1 teaspoon caraway or cumin seeds

1½ teaspoons baking soda

½ teaspoon baking powder

1 teaspoon sea salt

1 tablespoon honey

about 1½ cups buttermilk

an 8 x 4 x 2½-inch loaf pan, well greased

Makes 1 medium loaf

Preheat the oven to 350°F.

Put the flour, rye flakes, seeds, baking soda, baking powder, and salt in a large bowl and mix thoroughly. Make a well in the center. Put the honey and buttermilk in the well, then mix everything together with a wooden spoon to make a sticky, heavy dough. Flours vary, so if the dough is dry and hard to mix, add more buttermilk or regular milk 1 tablespoon at a time.

Sprinkle a few rye flakes in the base of the prepared loaf pan, then scrape the dough into the pan and spread evenly. Smooth the surface of the dough with a damp spatula or round-bladed knife and sprinkle a few more rye flakes over the top.

Bake for about 1 hour or until a skewer inserted into the center of the loaf comes out clean. Turn out the loaf onto a wire rack and let cool completely. Wrap tightly in foil or waxed paper and leave overnight before slicing.

Can be frozen for up to 1 month.

Variation: Raisin bread
Replace the seeds with 2 tablespoons raisins.

There's plenty of texture and taste in this dark, moist bread. It's particularly good spread with cream cheese for a satisfying snack or served with a platter of well-flavored cheeses—especially blue and goat cheeses—and a mixed salad.

pumpernickel and fig loaf

2 cups rye flour

1 cup regular whole-wheat flour or whole-wheat pastry flour

3 tablespoons wheat germ

3 tablespoons wheat bran

1½ teaspoons baking soda

½ teaspoon baking powder

1 teaspoon sea salt

1 tablespoon dark brown sugar

1 cup chopped dried figs

1½ cups buttermilk

1 extra-large egg

2 tablespoons molasses

2 tablespoons butter, melted

an 8 x 4 x 2½-inch loaf pan, well greased

Makes 1 medium loaf

Preheat the oven to 350°F.

Put the flours, wheat germ and bran, baking soda, baking powder, salt, and sugar in a large bowl and mix well with a wooden spoon. Stir in the figs, then make a well in the center of the ingredients.

In a separate bowl, beat the buttermilk with the egg, molasses, and melted butter. Pour into the well in the dry ingredients and mix to make a heavy and very sticky dough.

Scrape the dough into the prepared pan and spread evenly. Smooth the top of the loaf with a damp spatula or round-bladed knife. Bang the pan on the work surface a couple of times to remove any pockets of air, then bake for 55–60 minutes or until a skewer inserted into the center of the loaf comes out clean.

Loosen the loaf with a round-bladed knife, turn it out onto a wire rack, and let cool completely before slicing. Keep tightly wrapped and eat within 3 days. Can be frozen for up to 1 month.

The traditional bread of Ireland was made at home on the farm and baked in an iron pot suspended over a peat fire. The bread gets its light texture and superb flavor from mixing the creamy-white unbleached flour with buttermilk and baking soda. You can also make a brown bread variation, or a speckled loaf that uses the white bread recipe given here, with 4 oz of dark chocolate or chocolate chips (or raisins) and a tablespoon of sugar mixed into the dry ingredients.

Irish soda bread

3½ cups unbleached
all-purpose flour

1¼ teaspoons baking soda

1 teaspoon sea salt

about 1⅔ cups buttermilk

*a nonstick baking sheet, lightly
dusted with flour*

Makes 1 medium loaf

Preheat the oven to 425°F.

Sift the flour, baking soda, and salt into a large bowl and make a well in the center. Pour the buttermilk into the well and mix it into the dry ingredients with a round-bladed knife or your hands to make a soft, slightly sticky, rough-looking dough.

Turn out the dough on a lightly floured work surface and shape it into a ball. Set the dough onto the baking sheet and gently flatten it so it is about 1½ inches high. With a table knife score the dough with a cross. Dust with a little flour then bake for about 35 minutes until a good golden brown. To test if the loaf is cooked, tap underneath with your knuckles. If it sounds hollow, it is ready. If it gives a dull thud, bake it for a few minutes longer and test it again.

Transfer to a wire rack to cool. Wrap well to store or freeze for up to 1 month.

Variation: Brown soda bread

The traditionally used brown wheaten flour with its coarse flakes is hard to find outside Ireland, but a mix of 1½ cups whole-wheat flour (stone-ground, if possible), 1½ cups unbleached all-purpose flour, ⅓ cup wheat germ, and ⅓ cup wheat bran works well. Mix the flours, wheat germ, bran, 1¼ teaspoons baking soda, and 1 teaspoon salt together in a large bowl—don't sift them—add about 1½ cups buttermilk, then follow the method for the main recipe.

This nutritious loaf, bright green on the inside, is prepared in a few minutes in a food processor. It slices well and makes excellent sandwiches—it's also good with soups and salads.

watercress and arugula loaf

3½ cups self-rising flour

¼ teaspoon sea salt

a couple of grinds of black pepper

a handful of watercress sprigs (about 1 oz)

a small handful of arugula (about ½ oz)

1 cup cottage cheese

1 extra-large egg

about ⅓ cup milk (not fat-free)

an 8 x 4 x 2½-inch loaf pan, well-greased

Makes 1 medium loaf

Preheat the oven to 350°F.

Put the flour, salt, black pepper, watercress, and arugula in the bowl of a food processor. Run the machine until the leaves are fairly finely chopped. Add the cheese and the egg and run the machine until the ingredients are mixed roughly. Then, with the machine running, pour in the milk through the feed tube to make a fairly soft dough.

Scrape the dough into the prepared pan and with floured fingers press it into a neat loaf shape. With a sharp knife, cut a deep slash along the top of the loaf.

Bake for 40 minutes until a good golden brown. Remove the loaf from the pan and tap it underneath with your knuckles—if it sounds hollow the loaf is ready. If there is a dull thud, then bake for another 5 minutes and test again.

Turn out the loaf onto a wire rack and let cool completely before slicing. Wrap the loaf tightly and eat within 2 days, or toast. Can be frozen for up to 1 month.

My Sri Lankan neighbor, Jean, makes roti with grated fresh coconuts on special occasions, but this is her "quick" recipe. These thin breads are usually made with atta flour (chapatti flour), but whole-wheat pastry flour works well. Serve roti as a snack or with curries.

Sri Lankan coconut roti

1½ cups shredded unsweetened coconut

3 cups whole-wheat pastry flour or sifted fine whole-wheat flour

1 teaspoon baking powder

2 teaspoons sea salt

4 tablespoons unsalted butter, chilled and cut into cubes

1 small onion, very finely chopped

1 medium-hot fresh red chile, seeded and chopped

1 extra-large egg, lightly beaten

a heavy griddle or heavy skillet, lightly greased

Makes 12

Mix the coconut with 1 cup water in a large bowl and let soak for 20 minutes.

Meanwhile, in another bowl, mix the flour with the baking powder and salt. Add the cubes of butter and rub them in with the tips of your fingers until the mixture looks like fine crumbs. Stir in the chopped onion, chile and soaked coconut, followed by the egg, and mix with a round-bladed knife to make a soft dough. Flours vary, so if the mixture is dry and stiff, add a little water 1 teaspoon at a time. Cover the bowl and leave for 30 minutes.

Divide the dough into 12 equal pieces and shape each into a ball. Flatten and pat out each ball of dough to make a thin disk about 5½ inches across. Cover until ready to cook.

Put the greased griddle or skillet over medium heat. Cook the roti, one at a time, for about 2 minutes on each side until lightly flecked with brown. Keep warm in a low oven, covered, until ready to serve.

These naan are my children's favorite bread—they call them my puffy bread—and we have them for supper with curries once a week. The dough is simply mixed, left to rest, then shaped quickly and, when supper is ready, cooked under a very hot broiler and eaten straight away.

cracked pepper naan

2 cups self-rising flour

½ teaspoon coarsely ground black pepper or cracked black peppercorns

¼ teaspoon sea salt

2 generous tablespoons plain yogurt (not fat-free)

about ⅓–½ cup lukewarm water

4 tablespoons unsalted butter

2 garlic cloves, crushed

Makes 8
Serves 4

Mix the flour with the pepper and salt in a large bowl. Make a well in the center and add the yogurt. Add the water to the bowl a little at a time, working the ingredients together with your fingers to make a soft and slightly sticky dough. Work the dough in the bowl for a couple of seconds to make a ball.

Cover the bowl with a damp kitchen towel and set aside in a warm spot to ferment for about 1 hour.

When ready to cook, heat the broiler (and broiler rack) to its highest setting. Gently melt the butter with the garlic in a small pan or in the microwave.

Turn out the dough onto a lightly floured work surface and divide into 8 equal portions. With floured fingers, shape each piece into a ball then flatten and press it into an oval about 4½ x 3¼ inches.

Cook the naan, in batches, directly on the broiler rack under the heated broiler. As soon as the breads puff up and are light golden—about 2 minutes, depending on the heat of the broiler—flip them over using kitchen tongs and cook the second side until flecked with brown spots (about 1 minute). Remove from the broiler and brush the uppermost side with the hot melted butter and garlic. Wrap in a warm, clean cloth and serve immediately.

This bread is so-named because it was traditionally cooked in the bush by stockmen in the damped-down ashes of a campfire. The simple flour and water dough, sometimes enriched with bacon fat, was wrapped around a stick and cooked, or shaped into a round loaf and cooked in an iron pot buried in the hot ashes. Dampers were eaten with broiled, fried, or barbecued meat or spread with golden syrup—and are still very popular today with a younger generation.

Australian damper

2 cups self-rising flour

¼ teaspoon sea salt

2 tablespoons unsalted butter, chilled and cut into cubes

about ¾ cup milk (not fat-free) plus extra for brushing

a baking sheet, lightly greased

Makes 1 medium loaf

Preheat the oven to 375°F.

Mix the flour with the salt in a large bowl. Add the butter and rub it into the flour with the tips of your fingers until the mixture looks like fine crumbs.

Stir in the milk with a round-bladed knife to make a soft but not sticky dough. Turn the dough out of the bowl onto a lightly floured work surface and shape it into a nice soft, smooth ball.

Set the ball of dough onto the baking sheet and flatten it gently to make a round about 6½–7 inches across. With a sharp knife cut a deep cross in the dough then brush lightly with milk.

Bake for 30 minutes until golden. Transfer to a wire rack and let cool slightly. Serve warm or at room temperature. Best eaten within 2 days, or toasted. Can be frozen for up to 1 month.

Variations:
• Add 1⅓ cups grated sharp cheddar cheese to the mixture before adding the milk and sprinkle with a little extra cheese before baking. You can also add 2 tablespoons snipped chives or chopped parsley.
• Add 1 tablespoon golden syrup or light corn syrup and 2 tablespoons sugar to the mixture with the milk.
• Replace the milk with beer.

corn**breads**

Stone-ground yellow cornmeal gives this cornbread a wonderful texture, and the buttermilk and honey make for a soft, sweet crumb. For a change you could add 3 tablespoons toasted pine nuts, fresh or frozen corn kernels, or grated mature cheese.

buttermilk cornbread

1 cup fine yellow cornmeal, preferably stone-ground

1 cup unbleached all-purpose flour

1 ½ teaspoons baking powder

½ teaspoon baking soda

½ teaspoon sea salt

1 extra-large egg

4 tablespoons melted butter

3 tablespoons honey

1 cup buttermilk

an 8-inch square cake pan, well greased

**Makes 1 medium bread
6–8 portions**

Preheat the oven to 400°F.

Put the cornmeal, flour, baking powder, baking soda, and salt in a large bowl and stir with a wooden spoon until thoroughly mixed.

In a separate bowl, beat the egg with the melted butter, honey, and buttermilk. Stir into the dry ingredients to make a thick, smooth batter. Transfer the mixture to the prepared pan and spread evenly.

Bake for 15–20 minutes until golden and a toothpick inserted into the center comes out clean. Turn out onto a bread board, cut into large squares, and serve warm.

Best eaten the same day. Can be frozen for up to 1 month—gently warm before serving.

The bacon gives a wonderful flavor to this recipe. I prefer to use a dry-cured, smoked, streaky bacon, but everyone has a particular favorite. The same goes for the chile; put in just what you like and what will work best with other dishes. This cornbread is excellent eaten with a thick lentil or pea soup. You can bake the bread in the same pan you use to cook the bacon, or in a square pan.

spicy bacon cornbread

6 slices bacon, finely chopped

2 scallions, chopped

1 medium-hot chile pepper, or to taste, chopped

1 cup unbleached all-purpose flour

1 cup yellow cornmeal, preferably stone-ground

½ teaspoon baking soda

1 teaspoon baking powder

¼ teaspoon sea salt

1 cup buttermilk

1 tablespoon honey

1 extra-large egg

3 tablespoons melted butter

an 8-inch square cake pan, well greased, or a cast-iron ovenproof skillet about 9 inches across

Makes 1 medium bread
Serves 6–8

Preheat the oven to 400°F.

Put the chopped bacon in a cold skillet and cook gently until the fat begins to run and the bacon becomes golden and crisp. Stir in the chopped scallions and the chile, then remove the pan from the heat and set aside to cool.

In a large bowl, combine the flour, cornmeal, baking soda, baking powder, and salt.

In another bowl, beat together the buttermilk, honey, egg, and melted butter. Add this mixture to the dry ingredients and mix thoroughly with a wooden spoon. Stir in the cooled bacon, scallions, and chile from the skillet.

Scrape the mixture into the prepared cake pan or the greasy skillet and spread evenly.

Bake for 20 minutes until firm to the touch. Best eaten warm the same day. Can be frozen for up to 1 month—reheat thoroughly before serving.

This cornbread is usually baked in the oven in a heavy, cast-iron skillet. You can also use an ordinary cake pan or one of the huge range of fancy and rustic iron cornbread pans available. Hearty and satisfying, Southwest cornbread is good with salads as well as with broiled or barbecued meat and casseroles.

Southwest cornbread

2 cups corn kernels, fresh or frozen

⅔ cup fine yellow cornmeal, preferably stone-ground

1 teaspoon baking powder

½ teaspoon sea salt

½ cup pine nuts, toasted

1 rounded teaspoon chopped fresh sage leaves

1 scallion, sliced

1 cup unbleached all-purpose flour

¼ cup corn oil

2 extra-large eggs

1 cup buttermilk

a pat of butter

a 9-inch cast-iron, ovenproof skillet or an 8-inch square cake pan

Makes 1 medium bread
Serves 6–8

Preheat the oven to 350°F.

Put the corn kernels, cornmeal, baking powder, salt, pine nuts, sage, scallion, and flour in a large bowl and mix well.

In a separate bowl, beat the oil with the eggs and buttermilk, then stir into the dry ingredients to make a thick batter.

If you are using the skillet, heat the pan with the pat of butter in the oven until foaming—about 3 minutes. If you are using a cake pan, then grease it well.

Pour the batter into the hot skillet or the prepared pan and bake in the oven for about 20 minutes until firm to the touch and a toothpick inserted into the center comes out clean. Serve while still warm, either straight from the skillet or turned out of the pan onto a cutting board and cut into large squares.

Best eaten the same day. Not suitable for freezing.

breakfast **breads**

This fairly rich loaf is perfect for breakfast, brunch, or tea. It is equally good made with whole-wheat flour, and dark raisins instead of golden ones.

lemon, almond, and raisin loaf

1½ sticks unsalted butter, softened

½ cup sugar

grated peel of 1 unwaxed lemon

2 extra-large eggs, beaten

2 cups whole-wheat flour

2 teaspoons baking powder

a good pinch of salt

freshly squeezed juice of ½ lemon

about ½ cup milk

¾ cup chopped or slivered almonds

⅔ cup golden raisins

a 9 x 5 x 3-inch loaf pan, greased and base-lined with parchment paper

Makes 1 large loaf

Preheat the oven to 350°F.

Put the butter, sugar, and lemon peel in a large bowl, and beat with a wooden spoon or electric mixer until light and creamy. Gradually beat in the eggs.

Tip the flour, baking powder, and salt onto the mixture. Add the lemon juice and the milk and stir in with a metal spoon. Mix in the almonds (reserving 1 tablespoon for the top) and raisins. Transfer the mixture to the prepared pan and smooth the surface. Scatter the almonds over the top, then bake for about 50 minutes until golden and firm, and a skewer inserted in the center comes out clean. Leave to cool in the pan for 5 minutes, then carefully remove from the pan and place on a wire rack to cool completely.

Serve thickly sliced. Best eaten within 3 days. Can be frozen for up to 1 month.

The classic French honey spice loaf dates back to medieval times. It should be made with equal weights of honey and flour and flavored with *quatre épices*, a mix of spices usually available only in French food stores (but you can make your own, see note below). For a change, try this made with grated chocolate instead of almonds and candied peel.

pain d'épices

1⅔ cups unbleached all-purpose flour

¾ cup rye flour

2 teaspoons baking powder

¼ teaspoon sea salt

½ teaspoon ground cinnamon

½ teaspoon ground cloves

½ teaspoon *quatre épices*

⅔ cup almonds, finely chopped

¼ cup candied peel or crystallized ginger, finely chopped

¾ cup flavorful honey

2 extra-large egg yolks

5 tablespoons milk

an 8 x 4 x 2½-inch loaf pan, greased and base-lined with parchment paper

Makes 1 medium loaf

Preheat the oven to 350°F.

Sift both flours, baking powder, salt, and all the spices into a large bowl.

Using a wooden spoon, stir in the chopped almonds and candied peel. Make a well in the center of the ingredients. Add the honey (in cold weather it is easier to measure and combine the honey if you stand the jar in a bowl of warm water for a few minutes first), egg yolks, and milk to the bowl and stir well to make a thick, heavy batter.

Scrape the mixture into the prepared pan and smooth the surface. Bake for about 45 minutes until golden and a skewer inserted into the center comes out clean. Turn out onto a wire rack, remove the lining paper, and let cool.

Best eaten within 5 days, or can be frozen for up to 1 month.

Note: to make *quatre épices*, the late Jane Grigson suggested mixing 7 parts finely ground black pepper with 1 part each of ground cloves, ground ginger, and grated nutmeg. Store in a screw-top jar.

Variation: Pain d'épices au chocolat
Replace the almonds and candied peel or ginger with 3½ oz dark or bittersweet chocolate, grated or finely chopped. As soon as the loaf comes out of the oven, turn it out of the pan and pour over a warm glaze made by gently melting 2 oz dark or bittersweet chocolate with 3 tablespoons milk and 2 tablespoons sugar.

Warm, sticky, fragrant cinnamon buns are hard to resist but they take hours to make the "proper" way with a yeast dough. In this shortcut method the dough is mixed in a processor then the buns are shaped quickly and baked—all the flavor in less time.

quick cinnamon buns

2⅔ cups unbleached all-purpose flour

¼ teaspoon baking soda

2 teaspoons baking powder

¼ cup sugar

a good pinch of sea salt

4 tablespoons unsalted butter, chilled and cut into cubes

⅔ cup cottage cheese

3 tablespoons plain yogurt

about 2 tablespoons milk

For the filling:

4 tablespoons unsalted butter, very soft

⅓ cup packed light brown sugar

1½ teaspoons ground cinnamon

1 cup pecan pieces

an 11 x 7-inch jelly roll pan or an 8 x 8-inch baking pan, well-greased

Makes 12

Preheat the oven to 400°F.

To make the dough, put the flour, baking soda, baking powder, sugar, and salt in the bowl of a food processor. Run the machine just long enough to combine the ingredients. Add the cubes of butter to the bowl and run the machine until you have a sandy texture.

Add the cottage cheese, yogurt, and 1 tablespoon of the milk and run the machine until the ingredients come together to make a ball of soft dough. If there are dry crumbs or the dough seems dry and hard, add extra milk 1 tablespoon at a time.

Turn out the dough onto a lightly floured work surface and roll out to a rectangle about 12 x 9 inches.

Using a round-bladed knife, spread the soft butter evenly over the dough. Mix the brown sugar with the cinnamon and sprinkle over the butter. Finally, scatter over the pecan pieces.

Roll up the dough from one long side to resemble a jelly roll. Using a sharp knife, cut the roll into 12 even-sized slices. Arrange the buns, cut side up, in the prepared pan in 4 rows of 3, setting them slightly apart.

Bake for about 20 minutes until light golden brown. Remove the pan from the oven and set on a wire cooling rack. Let cool for a couple of minutes, then remove the buns from the pan, gently separate them and eat while still warm.

Best eaten the same day. These buns don't freeze very well.

A cheerful, colorful loaf that brightens up an ordinary day. It can be made with fresh or frozen cranberries, so you can enjoy this bread at any time of year. However, it would be ideal for Thanksgiving or Christmas, when it would work particularly well for the inevitable turkey and cranberry sauce sandwiches.

cranberry loaf

2 cups unbleached all-purpose flour

1 tablespoon baking powder

a good pinch of sea salt

1 tablespoon wheat germ

a pinch of cumin seeds (optional)

½ cup sugar

grated peel of ½ unwaxed orange

1 cup walnut or pecan pieces

2 tablespoons raisins

1 cup cranberries, fresh or frozen

2 extra-large eggs

4 tablespoons unsalted butter, melted

⅔ cup milk (not fat-free)

an 8 x 4 x 2½-inch loaf pan, greased and base-lined with parchment paper

Makes 1 medium loaf

Preheat the oven to 350°F.

Sift the flour, baking powder, and salt into a large bowl. Stir in the wheat germ, cumin (if using), sugar, orange peel, nuts (reserving 1 tablespoon for the top of the loaf), and raisins.

Put the cranberries in a food processor and chop roughly. Stir into the flour mixture and make a well in the center.

In a separate bowl, beat the eggs with the butter and milk and pour into the well. Mix everything together with a wooden spoon.

Scrape the mixture into the prepared pan and smooth the surface. Scatter the reserved nuts over the top of the loaf.

Bake for 45–50 minutes or until a skewer inserted into the center of the loaf comes out clean.

Carefully remove from the pan and let cool completely on a wire rack before cutting.

Best eaten within 3 days, or frozen for up to 1 month.

Blueberries, fresh or frozen, are now available all year round. They add a good sharp bite to this richly flavored gingerbread. Unlike most gingerbreads, which improve on keeping, this fruit version is best eaten straightaway.

old-fashioned blueberry gingerbread

1 cup blueberries, fresh or frozen

1¾ cups unbleached all-purpose flour

1 teaspoon baking soda

a good pinch of sea salt

1 tablespoon ground ginger

1 teaspoon ground cinnamon

1 teaspoon apple pie spice

⅔ cup packed light brown sugar

7 tablespoons unsalted butter

⅓ cup molasses

⅓ cup light corn syrup

1 extra-large egg

1¼ cups buttermilk

a 9 x 5 x 3-inch loaf pan, greased and base-lined with parchment paper

Makes 1 large loaf

Preheat the oven to 350°F.

Toss the blueberries in 1 tablespoon of the measured flour and set aside. Sift the rest of the flour, the baking soda, salt, all the spices, and the sugar into a large bowl.

Gently melt the butter with the molasses and the corn syrup in a small pan over low heat.

In a separate bowl, beat the egg lightly with the buttermilk until just mixed.

Add the butter mixture to the flour mixture, then add the egg mixture. Mix thoroughly with a wooden spoon to make a smooth batter. Pour the mixture into the prepared pan, then scatter the blueberries evenly over the top.

Bake for 45–55 minutes, until firm to the touch and a skewer inserted into the center of the loaf comes out clean.

Set the pan on a wire rack and let cool before removing the gingerbread. Serve thickly sliced. Best eaten within a couple of days. This gingerbread doesn't freeze very well.

I've made a banana and walnut loaf for many years as a way of using up overripe fruit, but after tasting this loaf in San Francisco I couldn't wait to get home to try to adapt my recipe. The lime peel and juice add a Caribbean flavor. It's crucial to use unsweetened shredded coconut, long shred if possible.

banana and coconut loaf

¾ cup unsweetened shredded coconut

7 tablespoons unsalted butter, softened

½ cup packed light brown sugar

grated peel of 1 unwaxed lime

2 extra-large eggs, beaten

3 medium bananas, very ripe (about 1 cup peeled)

3 tablespoons plain yogurt (not fat-free)

2 cups unbleached all-purpose flour

1 teaspoon baking powder

½ teaspoon baking soda

a good pinch of sea salt

an 8 x 4 x 2½-inch loaf pan, greased and base-lined with parchment paper

Makes 1 medium loaf

Preheat the oven to 350°F.

Put the coconut in an ovenproof dish and toast in the heated oven for about 3 minutes until a light gold color. Let cool until needed.

Put the butter into a large bowl, add the sugar and the grated lime peel. Beat well with a wooden spoon or electric mixer. Gradually beat in the eggs.

Using a fork, mash the bananas fairly roughly so they keep a bit of texture. Add to the bowl together with the coconut. Halve the lime and squeeze out the juice, then add 1 tablespoon of the juice to the bowl with the yogurt. Mix in gently.

Set a strainer over the bowl and sift the flour, baking powder, baking soda, and salt onto the mixture. Mix in well, then scrape the mixture into the prepared pan and smooth the surface.

Bake for about 1 hour until golden and a skewer inserted into the center of the loaf comes out clean. Carefully remove from the pan and let cool on a wire rack. Serve thickly sliced. Best eaten within 3 days. Can be frozen for up to 1 month.

Variations:
• Banana and walnut loaf—omit the lime peel and juice and the coconut and add 1 teaspoon of pure vanilla extract and 1 cup walnut pieces.
• For more texture, use half all-purpose flour and half whole-wheat flour.

This light loaf has plenty of flavor and is good eaten with or without butter. Use a mixture of your favorite nuts—almonds, brazils, cashews, hazelnuts, pine nuts, walnuts, and pecans, but not peanuts.

fresh orange and nut loaf

1 cup unbleached all-purpose flour

1 cup whole-wheat flour

1½ teaspoons baking powder

¼ teaspoon baking soda

a good pinch of sea salt

a good pinch of grated nutmeg

a good pinch of ground cinnamon

½ cup packed light brown sugar

5 tablespoons unsalted butter, chilled and cut into cubes

grated peel of 1 unwaxed orange

1 cup chopped mixed nuts

1 extra-large egg, beaten

⅞ cup fresh orange juice (from 2–3 oranges)

an 8 x 4 x 2½-inch loaf pan, greased and base-lined with parchment paper

Makes 1 medium loaf

Preheat the oven to 350°F.

Put the flours, baking powder, baking soda, salt, spices, and sugar in a large bowl and mix.

Add the butter and rub it in with the tips of your fingers until the mixture looks like fine crumbs.

Stir in the grated orange peel and the nuts. In a separate bowl, mix the egg with the orange juice, then stir into the dry ingredients with a wooden spoon. Transfer the mixture to the prepared pan and smooth the surface.

Bake for about 50 minutes until golden and a skewer inserted into the center of the loaf comes out clean. Carefully turn out of the pan, remove the lining paper, and let cool on a wire rack.

Serve thickly sliced. Best eaten within 3 days. Can be frozen for up to 1 month.

A funny old recipe made in a saucepan. Dried vine fruits—dark and golden raisins, currants (plus chopped, mixed peel, if you are using a bag of ready-made dried fruit mix)—are plumped up and infused with strong tea on top of the stove to make a moist and deliciously rich loaf. Serve thickly sliced, with or without butter, and a good cup of tea.

blacksmith's tea loaf

1¼ cups strong black tea

1 stick unsalted butter

2 cups mixed dried fruit

2 teaspoons apple pie spice

½ cup packed light brown sugar

1 teaspoon baking soda

¼ teaspoon sea salt

1¾ cups whole-wheat flour

1 teaspoon baking powder

2 extra-large eggs, beaten

an 8 x 4 x 2½-inch loaf pan, greased and base-lined with parchment paper

Makes 1 medium loaf

Preheat the oven to 350°F.

Put the tea in a saucepan (nonaluminum) large enough to hold all the ingredients. Add the butter, fruit, spice, sugar, baking soda, and salt. Set over medium heat and bring to a boil, then reduce the heat and simmer gently for 5 minutes, stirring occasionally. Remove the saucepan from the heat and let cool for a couple of minutes.

Add the flour and baking powder to the saucepan and mix briefly, then stir in the eggs. When thoroughly mixed, scrape the mixture into the prepared loaf pan and smooth the surface.

Bake for about 40 minutes until firm to the touch and a skewer inserted into the center comes out clean. If the skewer comes out sticky, then bake for another 5 minutes and test again. Let cool, then turn out and remove the lining paper. Cut into thick slices to serve. The flavor is even better if the loaf is wrapped in foil or waxed paper and left overnight before cutting. Best eaten within 4 days. Can be frozen for up to 1 month.

Note: for special treats, make the loaf with a bag of luxury fruit mix, which includes candied cherries, dried pineapple, and apricots.

small **breads**

For an easy brunch or late dinner I like to bake popovers in flexible muffin molds or nonstick muffin tins, rather than the normal huge popover tins, and add a chunk of goat cheese and a dash of chile. The batter takes just a minute to make in a food processor. You can use your favorite goat cheese—mild and creamy or slightly aged and drier with a stronger flavor. Serve the popovers with a large salad.

popovers with goat cheese and chile

1 cup milk (not fat-free)

1 cup unbleached all-purpose flour

¼ teaspoon sea salt

1 tablespoon wheat germ

3 extra-large eggs

2 tablespoons unsalted butter, melted

5–6 oz goat cheese

1 medium-hot chile (or to taste), finely chopped

12-cup muffin tin, or flexible molds set on a baking sheet, well buttered

Makes 12
Serves 4–6

Preheat the oven to 425°F.

Put the milk, flour, salt, wheat germ, eggs, and melted butter in a food processor and run the machine until you get a smooth batter.

Cut the goat cheese into 12 fairly even pieces.

Pour the batter into the cups in the muffin tin so each cup is about half full. Add a piece of cheese to each and a little of the chopped chile.

Bake immediately for 25 minutes then—without opening the oven door—turn down the heat to 350°F and bake for a further 15 minutes. Serve straight from the oven.

Split and spread with butter, scones are the perfect companions for a big pot of tea or coffee. This recipe is very quick and easy. For the best taste, use unsalted butter, pure maple syrup (rather than a maple-flavored substitute), and pecans from a fresh pack.

maple pecan scones

2 cups unbleached
all-purpose flour

4 teaspoons baking powder

a good pinch of sea salt

4 tablespoons unsalted butter,
chilled and cut into cubes

1 cup pecan pieces

1 extra-large egg

¼ cup pure maple syrup

about 3 tablespoons milk

a baking sheet, greased

**Makes 1 scone round
Serves 6**

Preheat the oven to 425°F.

Sift the flour, baking powder, and salt into a large bowl. Add the butter and rub it in with the tips of your fingers until the mixture resembles fine crumbs. Mix in the pecans.

In a separate bowl, beat the egg with the maple syrup and 1 tablespoon of the milk. Stir into the flour mixture with a round-bladed knife to make a soft, coarse-looking dough. If the dough is dry and crumbly and won't stick together, stir in more milk 1 tablespoon at a time. If the dough is very wet and sticky, work in another tablespoon of flour.

Tip out the dough onto a work surface lightly dusted with flour and gently work it with your hands for a few seconds so it looks smoother. Put the dough ball onto the prepared baking sheet. Dip your fingers in flour and pat out the dough to a round about 1¼ inches thick and 7 inches across. Using a knife, cut the round into 6 wedges, but do not separate the dough before baking.

Bake for 18–20 minutes until light golden brown. Transfer to a wire rack and leave until the wedges are cool enough to separate. Serve warm the same day. The cooled scones can be wrapped tightly and frozen for up to 1 month.

Variation: Apple scone round
Make up the scone mixture, replacing the maple syrup with ¼ cup granulated sugar, and adding about 3 tablespoons more milk plus 1 large, tart eating apple (or 2 small to medium ones) peeled, cored, and chopped. Before baking, lightly brush the top of the scone round with milk and sprinkle over a little coarse grain sugar.

These tiny rounds of dough, flavored with chopped scallions, sun-dried tomatoes, or herbs, are made and baked in minutes. Serve as an appetizer, with olives, salami, prosciutto, soft cheese, and your favorite antipasti from the Italian deli.

little scallion breads

1 cup self-rising flour

¼ teaspoon sea salt

3 grinds of black pepper

2 medium scallions, finely chopped

2 tablespoons olive oil

1 extra-large egg

2 teaspoons sesame seeds

a 2-inch cookie cutter

a baking sheet, lightly greased

Makes 12 tiny rounds
Serves 6 as an appetizer

Preheat the oven to 375°F.

Mix the flour with the salt, pepper, and scallions in a large bowl. In a separate bowl, beat the olive oil with the egg and 1 tablespoon water, then add to the dry ingredients. Work the mixture with your hands to make a soft dough. If there are dry crumbs in the bowl, add more water 1 teaspoon at a time.

Turn out the dough onto a lightly floured work surface and knead for 10 seconds to make a smooth ball. Cover with a damp cloth and leave for a couple of minutes. Knead for a couple more seconds, then roll out to about ¼-inch thickness. Stamp out rounds with the cutter and set slightly apart on the baking sheet. Gather up the trimmings, re-roll, then cut out more rounds. Sprinkle with the sesame seeds and bake for 8–10 minutes until golden brown and firm to the touch.

Serve warm from the oven. Best eaten the same day. Can be frozen for up to 1 month; gently warm them before serving.

Variations:
Omit the scallions and use either 1 rounded tablespoon chopped sun-dried tomatoes or 1 tablespoon snipped chives or chopped flatleaf parsley.

Eaten hot, split, and spread with butter and jam, these "dropped" biscuits bring back memories of trips I have made to the southern states. For a light crumb, handle the dough as little as possible, barely enough to combine the ingredients. For savory biscuits to eat with thick soups and stews, add 2 oz chopped ham or salami, or crumbled cooked bacon to the mixture before the buttermilk.

fluffy buttermilk biscuits

2 cups unbleached all-purpose flour, plus extra for dusting

1 tablespoon baking powder

½ teaspoon baking soda

½ teaspoon sea salt

2 teaspoons sugar

3 tablespoons unsalted butter, chilled and cut into cubes

about 1 ⅓ cups buttermilk

a little melted butter for brushing

a baking sheet, lightly greased

Makes 12

Preheat the oven to 450°F.

Sift the flour, baking powder, baking soda, salt, and sugar into a large bowl.

Add the butter and rub it in with the tips of your fingers until the mixture looks like fine crumbs. Make a well in the center and pour in the buttermilk. Using a round-bladed knife quickly and briefly stir the ingredients together to make a really rough-looking, damp dough that will fall off a spoon.

Take 1 heaping tablespoon of the dough and drop it onto the baking sheet to make a rough mound. Repeat with the rest of the dough, spacing the mounds about 1 inch apart—they will spread in the oven so the sides will touch.

Dust lightly with flour, then brush with melted butter and bake for 12–15 minutes until golden and firm to the touch. Transfer carefully to a wire rack and leave until cool enough to handle, then separate and serve warm.

Best eaten the same day or gently reheated the next day. Can be frozen for up to 1 month.

Sour cream is the key to fine-tasting, rich, and moist bran muffins. My mother-in-law gave me another tip: they taste even better if you let the bran mixture soak for a while before baking. To make fruit muffins, replace the pecan nuts with fresh or frozen blueberries or pitted, chopped dates. This recipe makes muffins of a manageable size, not the giants you see in some coffee shops.

old-fashioned maple bran muffins

1 cup sour cream

½ cup milk (not fat-free)

1⅔ cups wheat bran

⅓ cup wheat germ

1 extra-large egg, beaten

¼ cup pure maple syrup

1 cup unbleached all-purpose flour

1 teaspoon baking powder

½ teaspoon baking soda

a pinch of sea salt

1 cup pecan pieces

a little coarse sugar for sprinkling

12-cup muffin tin lined with paper muffin cases, or a flexible mold tray

Makes 12 medium muffins

In a large bowl combine the sour cream with the milk, then stir in the wheat bran and the wheat germ and let soak for 30 minutes.

Meanwhile, heat the oven to 350°F.

Stir the egg and maple syrup into the sour cream mixture. Sift the flour, baking powder, baking soda, and salt onto the mixture and mix in. Stir in the pecans.

Spoon the mixture into the muffin cups to fill them evenly. Sprinkle each muffin with a little sugar then bake for about 25 minutes until firm to the touch.

Carefully turn out onto a wire cooling rack. Eat the same day while still warm, or the next day gently reheated. Can be frozen for up to 1 month.

It's difficult to think of more homey and comforting food than these small potato breads, fried in butter until they are crisp and golden outside and steaming and soft inside. Serve them along with a pile of fried bacon and just-cooked eggs.

Irish potato bread

1¾ cups smooth mashed potatoes (1 very large cooked potato or 2 medium)

¾ cup self-rising flour

¼ teaspoon powdered mustard

½ teaspoon sea salt

several grinds of black pepper

1 tablespoon snipped chives or 2 tablespoons chopped parsley

1 extra-large egg, beaten

a little butter for frying

a large heavy skillet

Makes 8
Serves 4

Mix the mashed potatoes with the flour, mustard, salt, pepper, and herbs—do this with a wooden spoon, not a food processor (otherwise you'll get a gluey mess).

Work in the beaten egg to make a firm dough. If it is very soft and sticky work in a little more flour.

Turn out the dough onto a floured work surface, flour your hands, then knead the dough once or twice to make a smooth ball. Divide the dough into 8 equal portions and shape each one into a small cake about 2½ inches across.

When ready to cook, heat a little butter in a large heavy skillet, preferably nonstick, and cook the breads over medium heat for about 7 minutes on each side until a good golden brown and slightly puffed. Serve immediately.

Variation:
Add 1⅓ cups grated sharp cheddar cheese before adding the egg.

I discovered the best apple doughnuts at a roadside cider-apple press and store in Bartlett, New Hampshire, and have been experimenting to recreate the taste for a couple of years. This quick recipe is based on a rich potato-scone dough, introduced to New England by Irish farmers, which makes excellent, light, and well-flavored doughnuts.

cider-apple doughnuts

2 medium-tart eating apples

1 teaspoon ground cinnamon

3⅓ cups unbleached all-purpose flour

¼ teaspoon sea salt

1 tablespoon baking powder

1 cup sugar

3 tablespoons unsalted butter, chilled and cut into cubes

1 cup smooth mashed potatoes (1 large cooked potato or 2 small), at room temperature

2 extra-large eggs, beaten

½–¾ cup milk (not fat-free)

To finish:

safflower or canola oil for deep-frying

2 tablespoons sugar

1 teaspoon ground cinnamon

a doughnut cutter, or 3-inch round pastry cutter and ½-inch round pastry cutter; deep-fat fryer or large deep saucepan

Makes 12

Peel, core, and chop the apples into small pieces, about the size of your little fingernail. Sprinkle with the cinnamon and toss until thoroughly mixed. Set aside until needed.

Sift the flour, salt, baking powder, and sugar into a large bowl. Add the butter and rub it in with the tips of your fingers until the mixture looks like fine crumbs. Work in the mashed potatoes, then stir in the apple mixture with a round-bladed knife. Add the eggs and enough milk to make a soft but not sticky scone-like dough.

Turn out the dough onto a lightly floured work surface and pat it out to about ¾ inch thick. Cut into rounds with the doughnut cutter, or use the large pastry cutter and then stamp out the center rounds with the smaller cutter. Gather up the trimmings and pat them out to make more doughnuts.

Heat the oil in a deep-fat fryer or large deep saucepan to 350°F or until a cube of bread turns golden in 40 seconds. Fry the doughnuts in batches for 5–6 minutes, turning them frequently, until a good golden brown. Remove with a slotted spoon and drain on paper towels. Toss in the sugar mixed with the cinnamon and let cool before eating. Best eaten the same day. These doughnuts are not suitable for freezing.

index

almonds:
  lemon, almond, and raisin
    loaf, 35
  pain d'épices, 36
apples:
  apple scone round, 52
  cider-apple doughnuts,
    63
arugula, watercress and
  arugula loaf, 21
Australian damper, 26

banana and coconut loaf,
  44
blacksmith's tea loaf, 48
blueberry gingerbread, 43
breakfast breads, 35–49
brown soda bread, 18
bulghur wheat, seedy loaf,
  10
buns, quick cinnamon, 39
buttermilk:
  buttermilk cornbread, 29
  fluffy buttermilk biscuits,
    56
  Irish soda bread, 18
  molasses oatmeal loaf,
    13
  old-fashioned blueberry
    gingerbread, 43
  pumpernickel and fig
    loaf, 17
  quick rye bread, 14
  Southwest cornbread, 33
  spicy bacon cornbread,
    30

cheese:
  popovers with goat
    cheese and chile, 51
  quick cinnamon buns, 39
  watercress and arugula
    loaf, 21
chiles:
  popovers with goat
    cheese and chile, 51
  Sri Lankan coconut roti,
    22
chocolate, pain d'épices au
  chocolat, 36
cider-apple doughnuts, 63
cinnamon buns, 39
coconut:
  banana and coconut loaf,
    44
  Sri Lankan coconut roti,
    22
cornbreads, 29–33
  buttermilk cornbread 29
  Southwest cornbread, 33

spicy bacon cornbread,
  30
cracked pepper naan, 25
cranberry loaf, 40

damper, Australian, 26
doughnuts, cider-apple, 63
dried fruit, blacksmith's tea
  loaf, 48

figs, pumpernickel and fig
  loaf, 17
fluffy buttermilk biscuits,
  56

gingerbread, old-fashioned
  blueberry, 43
goat cheese, popovers with
  chile and, 51

honey, pain d'épices, 36

Irish potato bread, 60

lemon, almond and raisin
  loaf, 35

maple syrup:
  maple pecan scones, 52
  old-fashioned maple
    bran muffins, 59
molasses:
  molasses oatmeal loaf,
    13
  old-fashioned blueberry
    gingerbread, 43
  pumpernickel and fig
    loaf, 17
muffins, old-fashioned
  maple bran, 59

naan, cracked pepper, 25
nuts:
  fresh orange and nut
    loaf, 47
  see also almonds,
    walnuts etc

oatmeal loaf, molasses, 13
old-fashioned blueberry
  gingerbread, 43
old-fashioned maple bran
  muffins, 59
olive and rosemary bread,
  9
olive oil, Tuscan fresh sage
  and olive oil bread, 9
orange and nut loaf, 47

pain d'épices, 36

pecan nuts:
  cranberry loaf, 40
  maple pecan scones, 52
  old-fashioned maple
    bran muffins, 59
  quick cinnamon buns, 39
pepper, cracked pepper
  naan, 25
popovers with goat cheese
  and chile 51
potatoes:
  cider-apple doughnuts,
    63
  Irish potato bread, 60
pumpernickel and fig loaf,
  17

raisins:
  cranberry loaf, 40
  lemon, almond, and raisin
    loaf, 35
  raisin bread, 14
roti, Sri Lankan coconut,
  22
rye flour:
  pain d'épices, 36
  pumpernickel and fig
    loaf, 17
  quick rye bread, 14

sage:
  Tuscan fresh sage and
    olive oil bread, 9
savory breads, 9–27
scallion breads
scones:
  apple scone round, 52
  maple pecan scones, 52
seedy loaf, 10
small breads, 51–63
soda bread, Irish, 18
Southwest cornbread, 33
spicy bacon cornbread, 30
Sri Lankan coconut roti, 22

tea loaf, blacksmith's, 48
Tuscan fresh sage and
  olive oil bread, 9

walnuts:
  banana and walnut loaf,
    44
  cranberry loaf, 40
  seedy loaf, 10
  watercress and arugula
    loaf, 21
wheat flakes, seedy loaf,
  10

yogurt, seedy loaf, 10

conversion chart

Weights and measures have been rounded up
or down slightly to make measuring easier.

Volume equivalents:

American	Metric	Imperial
1 teaspoon	5 ml	
1 tablespoon	15 ml	
¼ cup	60 ml	2 fl.oz.
⅓ cup	75 ml	2½ fl.oz.
½ cup	125 ml	4 fl.oz.
⅔ cup	150 ml	5 fl.oz. (¼ pint)
¾ cup	175 ml	6 fl.oz.
1 cup	250 ml	8 fl.oz.

Weight equivalents: Measurements:

Imperial	Metric	Inches	Cm
1 oz.	25 g	¼ inch	5 mm
2 oz.	50 g	½ inch	1 cm
3 oz.	75 g	¾ inch	1.5 cm
4 oz.	125 g	1 inch	2.5 cm
5 oz.	150 g	2 inches	5 cm
6 oz.	175 g	3 inches	7 cm
7 oz.	200 g	4 inches	10 cm
8 oz. (½ lb.)	250 g	5 inches	12 cm
9 oz.	275 g	6 inches	15 cm
10 oz.	300 g	7 inches	18 cm
11 oz.	325 g	8 inches	20 cm
12 oz.	375 g	9 inches	23 cm
13 oz.	400 g	10 inches	25 cm
14 oz.	425 g	11 inches	28 cm
15 oz.	475 g	12 inches	30 cm
16 oz. (1 lb.)	500 g		
2 lb.	1 kg		

Oven temperatures:

110°C	(225°F)	Gas ¼
120°C	(250°F)	Gas ½
140°C	(275°F)	Gas 1
150°C	(300°F)	Gas 2
160°C	(325°F)	Gas 3
180°C	(350°F)	Gas 4
190°C	(375°F)	Gas 5
200°C	(400°F)	Gas 6
220°C	(425°F)	Gas 7
230°C	(450°F)	Gas 8
240°C	(475°F)	Gas 9